PUERTO RICO 2025

A complete guide to the island's top destinations, culture and hidden gems.

By
Santiago Cruz

COPYRIGHT

© 2024 by Santiago Cruz

All rights reserved. No part of this book may be reproduced or transmitted in any form without permission from the author or publisher, except for brief quotes used in reviews or articles.

TABLE OF CONTENT

COPYRIGHT 2
TABLE OF CONTENT 3
INTRODUCTION 7
    About This Guide 7
    Why Puerto Rico? 8
    How To Use This Book 9
    What's New In 2025 10
CHAPTER 1 13
WELCOME TO PUERTO RICO 13
    A Snapshot Of Puerto Rico 13
    Why Travel To Puerto Rico In 2025? 15
    Recent Developments And Trends 18
CHAPTER 2 21
ESSENTIAL TRAVEL INFORMATION 21
    COVID-19 Guidelines and Health Precautions ... 21
    Entry Requirements And Visa Information 23
    Currency, Language, And Local Etiquette 24
CHAPTER 3 27
BEST TIMES TO VISIT 27
    Seasons And Weather 27

Major Festivals And Events In 2025................ 31
CHAPTER 4.. 34
GETTING TO PUERTO RICO AND MOVING AROUND.. 34
Flights And Ferry Services............................... 34
Transportation Around Puerto Rico............... 37
Rental Cars.. 37
Public Transit.. 38
Rideshare Services and Taxis........................... 39
Other Options... 40
Insider Tips For Navigating Puerto Rico.......... 41
CHAPTER 5... 43
PLANNING YOUR TRAVEL BUDGET......... 43
Accommodation Expenses................................43
Food And Dining Costs................................... 45
Activity Costs.. 47
Shopping And Souvenirs................................. 48
Tips For Budgeting..49
CHAPTER 6... 51
ACCOMMODATION....................................... 51
Top Accommodations By Region..................... 51
Luxury Stays... 52
Mid-Range Accommodations........................... 52
Budget-Friendly Stays......................................53
Alternative Stays: Eco-Lodges, Glamping, and

Local Guesthouses..57
CHAPTER 7.. **59**
EXPLORING SAN JUAN AND ITS SURROUNDINGS.. **59**
   Old San Juan: A Window Into The Past............ 60
   Condado and Isla Verde: Sun, Sand, and Entertainment... 64
   Other Highlights Around San Juan................. 67
CHAPTER 8.. **69**
DISCOVERING PUERTO RICO'S EAST COAST AND ISLANDS................................. **69**
   El Yunque Rainforest: A Tropical Gem............70
   Vieques And Culebra: Island Getaways............74
   Culebra: Paradise For Beach Lovers..................77
   Tips For Visiting The Islands............................79
CHAPTER 9.. **81**
EXPLORING THE SOUTH COAST OF PUERTO RICO... **81**
   Ponce: The "Pearl Of The South"...................... 82
   Guanica Dry Forest: A Rare Ecosystem............ 85
   Tips For Your South Coast Adventure..............87
CHAPTER 10.. **88**
EXPLORING PUERTO RICO'S WEST COAST..**88**
   Rincon: Surfing And Stunning Sunsets.......... 89
   Cabo Rojo: Nature's Masterpiece..................... 92

Tips For Visiting The West Coast........................ 95
CHAPTER 11 .... **97**
EXPLORING PUERTO RICO'S CENTRAL MOUNTAINS... **97**
    Utuado: Coffee Farms And Outdoor Adventures 98
    Jayuya: Indigenous History and Scenic Views 102
    Tips For Visiting The Central Mountains....... 106
CHAPTER 12 .... **108**
STAYING SAFE IN PUERTO RICO.............. **108**
    Safety Tips For Solo Travelers, Families, And Couples... 108
    Common Scams And How To Avoid Them.. 111
    General Safety Tips For Puerto Rico................ 114
CHAPTER 13 .... **115**
PACKING AND GETTING READY............. **116**
    What To Pack For Different Activities............ 116
    Travel Insurance And Emergency Contacts....119
    Extra Packing Tips..120
CHAPTER 14... **121**
UNDERSTANDING PUERTO RICAN CULTURE... **122**
    Simple Spanish Phrases For Visitors................ 122
    Tips For Puerto Rican Etiquette...................... 125
CHAPTER 15... **128**

SAMPLE ITINERARIES.................... 128
   3-Day Weekend in San Juan.................... 129
   5-Day East Coast Adventure.................... 132
   7-Day Island Road Trip.................... 133
   14-Day Full Puerto Rico Experience.................... 134
CHAPTER 16.................... 135
HELPFUL CONTACTS AND WEBSITES... 135
   Tourist Information Centers.................... 136
   Emergency Numbers And Services.................... 139
   Tourism And Safety Assistance.................... 141
CONCLUSION.................... 141

INTRODUCTION

About This Guide

Welcome to Puerto Rico 2025: A complete guide to the island's top destinations, culture and hidden gems. Whether it's your first trip to this stunning island or you're coming back to explore more, this guide is here to help you uncover all that Puerto Rico has to offer.

Puerto Rico isn't just another tropical destination—it's a place filled with culture, history, natural wonders, and friendly people. This book will make your trip planning easy and help you enjoy your stay, whether you're relaxing on beautiful beaches, hiking through lush rainforests, or diving into the island's lively city life.

Here's what you'll find inside:
- Helpful tips to make your trip stress-free.

- Recommendations on where to stay, eat, and explore.

- Sample travel plans for adventurers, families, and everyone in between.

- A closer look at Puerto Rico's unique culture, history, and regions.

Get ready to experience Puerto Rico in a way that's fun, memorable, and hassle-free!

Why Puerto Rico?

Puerto Rico, known as the "Island of Enchantment," is a mix of adventure, relaxation, and rich culture. Here's why it's such a special place to visit:

1. Breathtaking Nature
The island's landscapes are incredibly diverse. You can enjoy peaceful beaches like Flamenco Beach in Culebra, admire the cliffs at Cabo Rojo, hike in El Yunque Rainforest, or explore the magical Camuy River Cave Park.

2. Fascinating Culture
Puerto Rico's history blends influences from its Taíno, Spanish, African, and American roots. Walk through the colorful streets of Old San Juan, visit

forts like El Morro, and enjoy traditional music such as bomba and plena.

3. Easy for Travelers
As a U.S. territory, Puerto Rico is a convenient destination for American travelers. U.S. citizens don't need a passport, English is widely spoken, and the currency is the U.S. dollar.

4. Delicious Food and Drinks
Foodies will love Puerto Rico! Try local dishes like mofongo, lechón, and fresh seafood. Don't forget to sample Puerto Rican coffee, tropical fruits, and the island's famous rum cocktails.

5. Perfect Anytime
With warm weather year-round and exciting festivals and events happening all the time, Puerto Rico is a great destination no matter when you visit.

How To Use This Book

This guide is designed to fit every type of traveler, whether you're planning a quick weekend getaway or a longer vacation. Here's what you can expect:

Chapters 1–5: Practical information to help you plan your trip, from budgeting and transportation to understanding Puerto Rican culture.

Chapters 6–11: A region-by-region look at the island's best spots, accommodations, and must-see attractions.

Chapters 12–16: Travel tips, packing guides, safety advice, and itineraries tailored to different travel needs.

This guide will give you everything you need to create the perfect trip, tailored to your interests and budget.

What's New In 2025

In 2025, Puerto Rico is more exciting than ever, with new additions making it an even better place to visit:

1. Fresh Places to Stay
There are new eco-friendly lodges, luxury resorts, and budget accommodations to suit all kinds of travelers. Many of these focus on sustainability, letting you enjoy nature responsibly.

2. Better Transportation
Improved ferry services make it easier to reach places like Vieques and Culebra. Roads around the island have been upgraded, making travel smoother and faster.

3. Upgraded Attractions
Historic sites in Old San Juan have been restored, and hiking trails in El Yunque have been improved. Tours to bioluminescent bays in Vieques and Fajardo are now more accessible and organized.

4. Exciting Food Scene
Puerto Rico's food culture is thriving with more farm-to-table restaurants, coffee shops, and breweries. You'll find new places to enjoy fresh, locally sourced dishes and drinks.

5. Focus on Sustainability
The island has taken steps to protect its natural beauty by promoting eco-tourism and supporting local businesses, ensuring that your visit leaves a positive impact.

6. New Experiences

Visitors can now enjoy cultural workshops in rural areas, adventure tours like night kayaking in glowing bays, and other unique activities that let you connect with Puerto Rico in a deeper way

CHAPTER 1

WELCOME TO PUERTO RICO

A Snapshot Of Puerto Rico

Situated in the Caribbean Sea, Puerto Rico is an island filled with stunning scenery, lively culture, and a history that spans centuries. Often called the Island of Enchantment, this tropical destination has something for everyone—from sandy beaches to lush mountains. Although it measures just 110 miles long and 35 miles wide, Puerto Rico offers an impressive range of experiences within its compact area.

The island's culture is a unique mix of influences from its Taíno, Spanish, African, and American heritage. This cultural blend is evident in its music, art, food, and celebrations. In Old San Juan, the brightly colored buildings and cobblestone streets transport visitors back in time, but Puerto Rico is far from stuck in the past. Modern cities buzz with trendy restaurants, bustling nightlife, and innovative attractions.

Every part of Puerto Rico has its own charm:

San Juan and Metro Area: The vibrant capital mixes history with modern convenience. Visitors can explore historic forts, shop in stylish districts, or relax at urban beaches like Condado.

Eastern Puerto Rico: Home to El Yunque rainforest and the glowing waters of bioluminescent bays, this area also includes the serene islands of Vieques and Culebra, perfect for those looking for peace and quiet.

Southern Puerto Rico: Known for sunny weather, this region features cultural hubs like Ponce, which boasts art museums, colonial architecture, and a welcoming waterfront.

Western Puerto Rico: Famous for surfing and a laid-back atmosphere, this region offers dramatic cliffs, pristine beaches, and picturesque sunsets.

Central Puerto Rico: For adventurers and nature lovers, the island's central mountains provide breathtaking coffee plantations, hidden waterfalls, and quaint mountain towns like Jayuya and Utuado.

Thanks to its warm climate year-round, Puerto Rico is a great destination no matter the season. But what truly sets it apart is the genuine hospitality of its people, making every visitor feel at home.

Why Travel To Puerto Rico In 2025?

Puerto Rico has always been a favorite Caribbean destination, but 2025 brings fresh reasons to visit.

1. A Story of Resilience

The island has overcome major challenges in recent years, including hurricanes and global disruptions. Today, Puerto Rico shines brighter than ever, with upgraded infrastructure, better tourist services, and a strong commitment to eco-friendly travel. Visiting in 2025 means witnessing this remarkable transformation while supporting its ongoing recovery.

2. A Rich Cultural Heritage

With over 500 years of history, Puerto Rico is a treasure trove of cultural experiences. Expanded programs and tours in 2025 give travelers deeper insights into the island's past. Explore ancient forts like El Morro, visit world-class museums, and enjoy Afro-Caribbean music and traditional dance performances.

3. Breathtaking Nature

Puerto Rico's diverse landscapes are unmatched. In 2025, improved trails and facilities allow visitors to better experience El Yunque rainforest, the island's famous bioluminescent bays, and protected wildlife reserves. Its beaches, often ranked among the best in the world, range from bustling shores like Luquillo to secluded spots like Flamenco Beach on Culebra.

4. Easy for U.S. Travelers

As a U.S. territory, Puerto Rico offers hassle-free travel for Americans. No passport is needed, the U.S. dollar is the local currency, and English is widely spoken. Additionally, expanded flight options in 2025 make the island even more accessible.

5. Festivals and Events Galore

The island's 2025 events calendar is packed with exciting activities:

- The San Sebastián Street Festival in January, filled with live music, parades, and local art.

- The Coffee & Chocolate Expo, where visitors can savor locally produced treats.

- Various Patron Saint Festivals, celebrated in towns across the island with food, music, and dancing.

6. Focus on Sustainability

In 2025, Puerto Rico is doubling down on eco-tourism. Many hotels, tours, and attractions emphasize protecting the environment, giving travelers more options to experience the island responsibly.

Recent Developments And Trends

Puerto Rico in 2025 is an ever-evolving destination with new additions to enhance your trip.

1. Better Places to Stay

- Eco-Friendly Lodges: Stay in solar-powered cabins near El Yunque or beachfront villas built with sustainability in mind.

- Luxury Resorts: Several new high-end hotels offer private beaches, gourmet dining, and spa services.

- Budget Options: Affordable yet stylish guesthouses and hostels cater to travelers on a budget.

2. Improved Transportation

- Ferries: Upgraded ferry services make it easier to reach Vieques and Culebra.

- Eco-Friendly Rides: Cities now offer electric scooters and bike rentals for exploring sustainably.

- Road Improvements: Smoother highways and better signage make road trips more enjoyable.

3. New and Improved Attractions

- Old San Juan Tours: Discover hidden gems and lesser-known stories with guided tours in the historic district.

- Outdoor Adventure Parks: Zipline and climbing parks in the central mountains cater to thrill-seekers.

- Protected Nature Reserves: Places like Cabo Rojo and La Parguera now have updated visitor centers and eco-conscious facilities.

4. A Growing Food Scene

Puerto Rico's culinary offerings continue to flourish in 2025:

- Enjoy food tours through cities like San Juan, tasting local dishes and tropical drinks.

- Take cooking classes to master traditional recipes like mofongo.

- Visit craft breweries and distilleries to sample Puerto Rico's famous rum and locally brewed beers.

5. Tech-Friendly Travel

- Use apps to find restaurants, book tours, and learn about local history.

- QR codes at attractions make it easier to access guides in different languages.

CHAPTER 2

ESSENTIAL TRAVEL INFORMATION

Planning a trip to Puerto Rico is easier when you know the basics. This section covers everything you need to ensure a safe, comfortable, and enjoyable visit to the Island of Enchantment. From health tips to understanding local customs, this guide will help you prepare for your journey.

COVID-19 Guidelines and Health Precautions

Puerto Rico has taken steps to ensure a safe environment for both locals and travelers. While many restrictions have eased in 2025, staying informed about health practices is still important.

1. Current COVID-19 Rules:

- **Vaccination and Testing:** Travelers are no longer required to show vaccination proof or a negative COVID-19 test. However, it's wise to double-check for updates before your trip.

- **Mask Use:** Masks are optional in most areas but recommended in crowded spaces like airports and public transport.

2. Health Tips for Travelers:

- Keep hand sanitizer handy and maintain good hygiene, especially in busy tourist spots.

- If you feel sick during your visit, seek medical help. Puerto Rico has excellent hospitals and clinics across the island.

3. Travel Insurance:
While not required, travel insurance with health coverage is strongly recommended. It can cover unexpected medical issues or trip disruptions.

4. Emergency Numbers:
For emergencies, call 911.

The Puerto Rico Department of Health has a helpline for any public health-related questions.

Entry Requirements And Visa Information

Puerto Rico is an accessible destination, especially for U.S. travelers. Here's what you need to know about entry and documentation.

1. For U.S. Citizens:
Since Puerto Rico is part of the U.S., American travelers don't need a passport. A government-issued ID like a driver's license is enough.

No visa is required for entry.

2. For Non-U.S. Citizens:
Visitors from Visa Waiver Program (VWP) countries can enter with an approved ESTA (Electronic System for Travel Authorization).

Travelers from other countries must have a valid U.S. visa.

Check with the nearest U.S. embassy or consulate for details on required documents.

3. Customs Rules:
Puerto Rico follows U.S. customs regulations. If you plan to bring food, plants, or other goods, ensure they comply with USDA rules.

Avoid bringing restricted items to prevent fines or confiscations.

4. Main Airports:
Most visitors arrive at Luis Muñoz Marín International Airport (SJU) in San Juan.

Regional airports like Rafael Hernández Airport (BQN) in Aguadilla and Mercedita Airport (PSE) in Ponce provide alternative entry points.

Currency, Language, And Local Etiquette

Understanding Puerto Rico's currency, language, and customs will make your visit smoother and more enjoyable.

1. Currency:

The U.S. dollar (USD) is the official currency.

Credit and debit cards are widely accepted, but small vendors and local markets often prefer cash.

ATMs are easy to find in cities and tourist areas but may be scarce in remote regions, so carry some cash just in case.

2. Language:
Puerto Rico's official languages are Spanish and English. Spanish is the primary language, but many locals in tourist areas speak English.

Learning basic Spanish phrases like "hola" (hello), "gracias" (thank you), and "¿cuánto cuesta?" (how much does it cost?) can enhance your interactions.

3. Social Etiquette:
Greetings: Puerto Ricans are friendly and welcoming. A handshake or a light cheek kiss (for acquaintances) is common.

Dining: Tipping is customary, with 15–20% being standard. Meals are seen as a time to relax and connect, so don't rush through dining experiences.

Dress Code: Casual attire is fine for most activities, but dress modestly for churches or formal events. Avoid wearing beachwear in non-coastal towns.

Photography: Always ask before photographing people, especially in rural or traditional settings.

4. Respect for Culture:
Puerto Ricans are proud of their history and traditions. Show respect by learning about the culture and avoiding unfavorable comparisons to mainland U.S. practices.

Attend local events or festivals to experience the island's vibrant community spirit firsthand.

Taking time to understand Puerto Rico's health guidelines, entry rules, and cultural practices ensures a hassle-free and rewarding trip. By respecting local customs and staying prepared, you can fully enjoy the beauty and hospitality that this Caribbean gem has to offer

CHAPTER 3

BEST TIMES TO VISIT

Choosing the right time to visit Puerto Rico can make a big difference in your experience. Factors like weather, tourist activity, and the island's many festivals and events can help you plan the perfect trip. This chapter breaks down Puerto Rico's seasons, weather, and top events in 2025 so you can decide the best time for your adventure.

Seasons And Weather

Puerto Rico's tropical climate ensures warm weather throughout the year, but slight changes in temperature and rainfall make each season unique.

Winter (December to February)
Winter is a favorite time for visitors looking to escape colder climates and enjoy Puerto Rico's warm, sunny weather.

Weather Details:

Daytime temperatures range from 80–85°F (27–29°C), with cooler nights, especially in the mountains. Rain is rare, making outdoor activities more enjoyable.

Top Activities:
Spend your days lounging on beaches like Flamenco or Condado, explore the trails in El Yunque National Forest, or stroll through Old San Juan without worrying about rain.

Tips for Visitors:
Since this is peak travel season, book your flights and accommodations early. Costs may be higher, but the excellent weather and holiday festivities make it worth the splurge.

Spring (March to May)
Spring is an ideal time to visit, offering great weather, fewer crowds, and blossoming landscapes.

Weather Details:
Temperatures rise slightly to around 82–87°F (28–31°C), with occasional short rain showers that refresh the environment.

Top Activities:
Tour coffee farms in the central highlands, try water sports like snorkeling and paddleboarding, or explore Puerto Rico's lush countryside.

Tips for Visitors:
Spring is less busy, so you can enjoy lower prices and fewer crowds. If you visit during Easter, don't miss the unique religious celebrations and processions.

Summer (June to August)
Summer is an energetic season filled with festivals and family vacations, though it's also the start of the rainy season.

Weather Details:
Summer is the hottest season, with temperatures between 85–90°F (29–32°C). Brief afternoon rain showers are common but don't last long.

Top Activities:
Visit the island's bioluminescent bays for a magical evening, enjoy beach parties, and cool off with water-based activities like jet skiing or diving.

Tips for Visitors:

Summer is popular with local families, especially in July. Make reservations early if you plan to visit hotspots like Vieques or Culebra.

Fall (September to November)
Fall is the quietest season, offering peaceful escapes for travelers willing to take a chance on rainy weather.

Weather Details:
Temperatures remain warm, averaging 84–88°F (29–31°C). Rain is more frequent, but sunny intervals are common.

Top Activities:
Explore cultural sites, enjoy farm-to-table dining experiences, and take day trips to less-visited towns like Cabo Rojo or Ponce.

Tips for Visitors:
Take advantage of lower travel costs during this off-peak season. Consider purchasing travel insurance, especially during hurricane season.

Major Festivals And Events In 2025

Puerto Rico is known for its lively festivals, showcasing the island's music, food, history, and culture. Here are some of the best events to attend in 2025.

Cultural Festivals

1. San Sebastián Street Festival (January)
Held in Old San Juan, this famous festival features parades, live music, artisan markets, and dancing. It's a vibrant way to experience Puerto Rican culture.

2. Discovery of Puerto Rico Day (November)
Celebrate the island's history with parades, cultural exhibits, and educational activities. This event honors Puerto Rico's heritage and traditions.

Music and Arts Events
1. Puerto Rico Heineken JazzFest (March)
Jazz enthusiasts will love this festival, which brings world-class musicians to perform in San Juan's open-air venues.

2. Casals Festival (February)

This classical music festival pays tribute to famed cellist Pablo Casals, featuring orchestral performances, chamber music, and solo recitals.

Food and Drink Festivals
1. Coffee & Chocolate Expo (September)
A must-visit for food lovers, this expo highlights the best coffee and chocolate creations from local producers, along with tastings and workshops.

2. Festival de la Piña Paradisíaca (June)
Celebrate all things pineapple with delicious food, refreshing drinks, and fun family activities in the coastal town of La Parguera.

Seasonal Highlights
1. Three Kings Day (January 6)
This cherished holiday includes parades, music, and traditional gift-giving. It's a wonderful time to see Puerto Rico's festive side.

2. Holiday Season (December)
Puerto Rico's Christmas celebrations are among the longest in the world, filled with music, dancing, feasts, and parrandas (caroling).

Insider Tips for Planning

- **Plan Around Festivals:** Puerto Rican festivals are vibrant and memorable. Scheduling your visit during an event can make your trip extra special.

- **Check the Weather:** While the island's weather is generally predictable, keeping an eye on local forecasts is helpful, especially during the rainy season.

- **Book in Advance:** Winter and festival periods are busy. Secure accommodations and tickets early to get the best options and prices.

CHAPTER 4

GETTING TO PUERTO RICO AND MOVING AROUND

Traveling to Puerto Rico and exploring its many attractions is simple and straightforward, thanks to its excellent flight connections, ferry services, and various transportation options on the island. This chapter explains how to reach Puerto Rico and the best ways to get around once you're there.

Flights And Ferry Services

Flights to Puerto Rico

Puerto Rico is a key travel destination in the Caribbean, with regular flights from the U.S., Europe, and Latin America.

1. Main Airports:
- **Luis Muñoz Marín International Airport (SJU):** Located near San Juan, this is the island's largest airport and serves the majority of international and domestic flights.

- **Rafael Hernández Airport (BQN):** Found in Aguadilla, this airport provides flights from selected U.S. cities and is perfect for accessing western Puerto Rico.

- **Mercedita Airport (PSE):** This smaller airport in Ponce offers regional flights and is convenient for visiting southern parts of the island.

2. **Flight Options:**
    - **From the U.S. Mainland:** Airlines like Delta, JetBlue, Southwest, and American Airlines provide direct flights from cities such as Orlando, Miami, and New York.

    - **From International Destinations:** Carriers like British Airways and Iberia connect Puerto Rico to Europe via Madrid and London, while flights from Latin America may route through Panama or the Dominican Republic.

3. **Tips for Booking:**

- Book early, especially for the busy winter and summer seasons, to secure the best prices.

- Check multiple travel websites for deals, and be flexible with your travel dates to save money.

Ferry Services

Ferry services are a practical way to visit nearby islands like Vieques and Culebra or travel to neighboring countries.

1. Ferries to Vieques and Culebra:

Ferries operate from Ceiba, a town east of San Juan, to the islands of Vieques and Culebra, which are famous for their beautiful beaches.

Tickets can be booked online or at the terminal, but it's best to buy them in advance, especially during holidays or weekends.

2. International Ferries:

Some private ferry companies offer routes to other Caribbean destinations, such as the Dominican Republic.

3. Travel Tips:

Arrive early at the ferry terminal to ensure a seat, as they can fill up quickly.

Be aware of weather-related delays, as schedules may change unexpectedly.

Transportation Around Puerto Rico

Puerto Rico offers several ways to get around, ranging from renting a car to using public transportation or rideshare apps.

Rental Cars

Driving is one of the best ways to explore Puerto Rico, giving you the freedom to visit attractions at your own pace.

1. Availability and Options:
- Major companies like Enterprise, Avis, and Hertz have offices at airports and in cities.
- Local agencies may offer cheaper rates but check reviews to ensure reliability.

2. Driving in Puerto Rico:

- The road network is generally good, though rural roads may be narrower or less paved.

- Traffic follows U.S. laws, and most signs are in Spanish.

- Gas stations are common and easy to find in urban areas.

3. Costs and Tips:

- Daily car rental rates range from $40 to $80, depending on the type of car.

- Reserve your vehicle ahead of time, especially during peak travel seasons.

- Make sure your insurance covers potential damages or accidents.

Public Transit

Public transportation in Puerto Rico is affordable but limited compared to larger countries.

1. Buses (Guaguas):

The AMA bus system operates in the San Juan area. Fares are budget-friendly, around $0.75 per ride.

Buses are a practical way to get around San Juan but less reliable for reaching other parts of the island.

2. Tren Urbano:
This urban train connects key areas in San Juan, such as Bayamón and Santurce.

It's useful for commuting within the metro area but doesn't cover regions outside the city.

3. Limitations:
Public transit options are scarce in rural areas, so you may need to rely on other means of transportation.

Rideshare Services and Taxis

Rideshare apps and taxis are convenient options, especially for short trips or when public transport is unavailable.

1. Rideshare Apps:
Uber is widely available in cities like San Juan and Ponce, offering an easy and cashless way to travel.

Prices are competitive, but expect higher rates during busy times.

2. Taxis:
Taxis are common in tourist hotspots, airports, and hotels.

Fares are either metered or based on flat rates for certain routes, such as from the airport to Old San Juan.

3. Tips for Using Rideshares and Taxis:
- Confirm the price with taxi drivers before starting your trip.

- Check Uber fare estimates during peak hours to avoid surprises.

Other Options

1. Scooters and Bikes:
Some cities have bike rental programs and electric scooter services, ideal for short trips or scenic rides along the coast.

2. Private Shuttles and Tours:
Many companies offer private shuttles to popular destinations like El Yunque or Vieques, which is convenient for groups or travelers without cars.

Insider Tips For Navigating Puerto Rico

- **Plan Ahead:** Use apps like Google Maps to check traffic and choose the best routes.

- **Keep Small Cash:** Some public transit options and taxis require cash payments.

- **Parking Rules:** Follow posted signs to avoid fines, and don't park in areas marked with "No Estacionar."

- **Expect Traffic:** Urban areas like San Juan can have heavy traffic during rush hours, so give yourself extra travel time.

With so many transportation choices, getting to and around Puerto Rico is easy and flexible. By planning your travel routes and picking the best options for your needs, you can focus on enjoying everything the island has to offer.

CHAPTER 5

PLANNING YOUR TRAVEL BUDGET

When visiting Puerto Rico, it's important to understand the various expenses you might encounter, such as accommodations, food, activities, and shopping. With some planning, you can make the most of your trip, whether you're going all-out on luxury or keeping things affordable. Here's a detailed guide to help you prepare your budget and enjoy the island to its fullest.

Accommodation Expenses

In Puerto Rico, you'll find accommodations for all types of travelers, from high-end resorts to budget-friendly options.

High-End Stays

Resorts: Luxury resorts like the Ritz-Carlton Reserve in Dorado Beach or the Fairmont El San Juan offer premium features such as fine dining, spa treatments, and beach access. Prices usually start around $400 per night and can go over $1,000 during busy seasons.

Private Villas: Villas with amenities like private pools and beachfront locations are available in places like Vieques and Rincon. These rentals can range from $600 to $2,000 a night.

Mid-Range Lodging

Hotels: Well-known hotel chains such as Hyatt Place and Courtyard by Marriott can be found in major cities like San Juan and Ponce, with nightly rates of $120–$250.

Paradores: These small, family-run inns are in scenic rural or coastal areas. They typically cost $100–$200 per night and offer a chance to experience Puerto Rican culture.

Affordable Options

Hostels and Guesthouses: Budget travelers can find accommodations for $20–$50 a night in places like Old San Juan or beach towns.

Vacation Rentals: Rooms or apartments on platforms like Airbnb often cost $40–$80 a night, while entire homes in quieter areas might start at $100.

Camping Opportunities

For nature lovers, camping is an option at sites like Flamenco Beach in Culebra or within El Yunque National Forest. Fees are typically $20–$30 per night, but you'll need a permit.

Seasonal Pricing

Peak Season (December to April): Prices are highest in winter and spring, especially around holidays like Christmas and Easter.

Off-Season (September to November): Accommodations are more affordable, but weather can be unpredictable during hurricane season.

Food And Dining Costs

Puerto Rico offers a variety of dining experiences, from street food to fine dining, catering to all budgets.

Affordable Eats ($5–$15 per meal)
Street Food: Sample Puerto Rican staples like alcapurrias (fried fritters), empanadillas, or pinchos (grilled skewers) for $2–$5 each.

Local Eateries: Small cafeterias, known as fondas, serve hearty meals like rice and beans with pork or chicken for $8–$12.

Bakeries: Breakfast options, such as sweet mallorcas and coffee, are available for under $5.

Mid-Range Dining ($15–$40 per meal)
Casual Restaurants: Enjoy traditional dishes like mofongo (plantain-based dish) or fresh seafood for $20–$30 per person.

Coastal Dining: Seafood specialties like ceviche or fried red snapper in towns like Fajardo or Rincon cost around $25–$35.

Fine Dining ($50–$150 per meal)
Upscale Restaurants: High-end spots like Marmalade in San Juan offer gourmet experiences for $75–$150 per person.

Farm-to-Table: Restaurants like Bacoa in Rio Grande serve multi-course meals with locally sourced ingredients for $50–$80.

Dining Tips

Look for happy hour deals on appetizers and drinks to save money.

Try local beverages like Medalla beer or Don Q rum, which are often cheaper than imported options.

Activity Costs

Puerto Rico is packed with exciting things to do, whether you prefer free activities or luxury experiences.

Free or Low-Cost Activities

Beaches: Many beaches, like Playa Flamenco and Luquillo, are free to visit, though parking might cost $2–$5.

Historic Sites: Visiting landmarks like El Morro or Castillo San Cristóbal costs under $10 or is free with a National Parks Pass.

Hiking: Trails in El Yunque National Forest, such as La Coca Falls or Mt. Britton Tower, are free.

Moderate-Priced Experiences ($30–$100)
Water Sports: Activities like snorkeling, paddleboarding, and kayaking are priced between $40 and $75.

Cultural Tours: Guided tours of coffee plantations or Old San Juan are usually $25–$50.

Bioluminescent Bays: Evening kayaking tours to the glowing bays cost $50–$100.

Luxury Activities ($150+)
Private Boat Tours: Half-day trips to nearby islands start at $400 for small groups.

Scuba Diving: Advanced diving excursions to coral reefs or shipwrecks range from $150 to $250.

Shopping And Souvenirs

Puerto Rico offers a mix of affordable souvenirs and luxury items to bring home.

Budget-Friendly Souvenirs ($5–$20)
- Keychains, magnets, and small crafts from local markets.

- Bags of Puerto Rican coffee or bottles of hot sauce.

Mid-Range Souvenirs ($25–$50)
- Handcrafted jewelry or artisan-made items.

- Bottles of premium Puerto Rican rum, such as Don Q or Bacardi Reserva.

Luxury Souvenirs ($100+)
- Intricately designed vejigante masks or original artwork from local artists.

- Custom pieces like handcrafted furniture or one-of-a-kind sculptures.

Tips For Budgeting

1. Plan Your Expenses: Set a daily budget for food, activities, and extras.

2. Use Public Transit: Save money by opting for buses or Uber over car rentals.

3. Focus on Free Attractions: Enjoy Puerto Rico's many free activities, such as beaches and hiking.

4. Splurge Strategically: Reserve your splurge experiences for special days.

5. Shop Local: Avoid tourist traps and shop where locals go for better prices.

CHAPTER 6

ACCOMMODATION

Picking the right place to stay in Puerto Rico can make your trip more enjoyable, whether you're after a fancy resort, a cozy guesthouse, or an eco-friendly lodge in the middle of nature. This chapter highlights the best places to stay on the island, focusing on popular spots like San Juan, Vieques, Culebra, and Ponce. It also introduces alternative accommodations, such as eco-lodges and glamping options, for a more unique stay.

Top Accommodations By Region

Puerto Rico offers many types of accommodations, each reflecting the unique vibe of its region. From the historic beauty of San Juan to the peacefulness of Vieques, every area has its own distinct options.

San Juan (Capital City)

San Juan is the lively heart of Puerto Rico, offering everything from luxurious hotels to charming guesthouses, plus easy access to historic sites, beaches, and nightlife.

Luxury Stays

Condado Vanderbilt Hotel:
This historic, upscale hotel in the Condado area offers oceanfront views, fine dining, and a luxurious spa. Prices usually range from $300 to $600 per night.

The St. Regis Bahia Beach Resort: A five-star resort near Rio Grande, featuring a beautiful beach, a golf course, and top-notch amenities. Rates are around $500 to $1,000 per night.

Mid-Range Accommodations

Hotel El Convento: A boutique hotel in Old San Juan, once a convent, now beautifully transformed with modern amenities. Rates start at $200 per night.

Sheraton Puerto Rico Hotel & Casino: A convenient hotel near the convention center, offering a rooftop pool and other amenities. Rates typically begin at $180 per night.

Budget-Friendly Stays

San Juan Hostel: Ideal for budget travelers, this hostel provides simple rooms close to Old San Juan and beaches. Dormitory beds start at $30 per night.

Casa Blanca Guest House: A cozy guesthouse located in a quieter area, offering affordable rooms with a laid-back feel. Rates range from $75 to $100 per night.

Vieques (Off the East Coast)
Vieques is known for its peaceful beaches and natural beauty, perfect for travelers looking for a quiet retreat.

Luxury Stays:
W Retreat & Spa Vieques Island: A luxury resort with beachfront views, private villas, a spa, and fine dining. Rates range from $400 to $700 per night.

Hix Island House: A modern, eco-friendly boutique hotel that blends with the island's surroundings. Prices typically range from $300 to $500.

Mid-Range Accommodations:
El Blok: A trendy hotel with modern design and a great restaurant, located in Isabel II. Rates range from $150 to $250 per night.

Vieques Hostel: A friendly, budget-friendly option with easy access to the beaches. Dormitory beds cost around $25–$35 per night, while private rooms range from $75–$150.

Budget Stays:
La Finca Vieques: A rustic guesthouse in the countryside offering affordable rooms in a peaceful setting. Rates start at $50 per night.

Culebra (A Small Island East of Puerto Rico)
Culebra is known for its stunning beaches and clear waters, making it a perfect place for those who prefer a laid-back atmosphere.

Luxury Stays:

Club Seabourne: A boutique resort with a relaxed vibe, a pool, and close access to the best beaches. Rates range from $250 to $400 per night.

Mid-Range Accommodations:
Mamacita's Guest House: A popular guesthouse for travelers looking for comfort and charm. Rates typically range from $100 to $150 per night.

Culebra Beach Villas: Family-friendly beachfront villas and apartments with prices ranging from $150 to $250 per night.

Budget Stays:
Culebra International Hostel: A budget-friendly hostel offering dormitory beds and private rooms. Dormitory beds start at $25 per night, with private rooms costing between $60–$100.

Ponce (Southern Puerto Rico)

Ponce is a culturally rich city with museums, historical sites, and nearby beaches, offering both charm and history.

Luxury Stays:

Ponce Plaza Hotel & Casino: A historic hotel with elegant rooms, a pool, and a casino. Rates range from $150 to $250 per night.

Hilton Ponce Golf & Casino Resort: A beachfront resort offering golf, a casino, and scenic views. Prices typically range from $180 to $350 per night.

Mid-Range Accommodations:
Hotel Melia Ponce: A boutique hotel blending old-world charm with modern amenities. Rooms start at $90–$150 per night.

Boutique Hotel Belgica: A stylish and affordable option in the center of Ponce, with rates ranging from $80 to $150 per night.

Budget Stays:
Hostel Ponce: A simple, budget-friendly hostel offering dormitory beds and a welcoming atmosphere. Rates begin at $25 per night.

Alternative Stays: Eco-Lodges, Glamping, and Local Guesthouses

For those seeking a unique experience, Puerto Rico offers several alternative accommodations that go beyond traditional hotels.

Eco-Lodges

Eco-lodges are perfect for those who want to enjoy nature while minimizing their impact on the environment.

The Rainforest Inn: Situated in El Yunque National Forest, this eco-lodge offers a peaceful escape with beautiful views and hiking opportunities. Rates range from $150 to $200 per night.

Finca Cialitos Eco-Lodge: Located in the mountains of Jayuya, this eco-lodge focuses on organic farming and sustainability. Prices range from $100 to $150 per night.

Glamping

Glamping combines the adventure of camping with the luxury of modern amenities.

Hacienda Carabali Glamping: Near El Yunque, this glamping site features luxury tents with comfortable beds and private bathrooms. Rates range from $150 to $250 per night.

CocoCay Glamping: Located on the beach in Vieques, this glamping site offers air-conditioned tents, gourmet meals, and private beach access. Prices start at $200 per night.

Local Guesthouses
For a more personal and authentic Puerto Rican experience, consider staying at a local guesthouse, which offers a homely and comfortable atmosphere.

Casa Isabel: A charming guesthouse in San Juan offering both modern and vintage touches. Rooms start at $80 per night.

La Terraza de San Juan: A cozy guesthouse with great views of the city, just a short walk from Old San Juan. Rates range from $60 to $90 per night.

CHAPTER 7

EXPLORING SAN JUAN AND ITS SURROUNDINGS

San Juan, the lively capital of Puerto Rico, offers a perfect mix of history and modern attractions. It's a hub where colonial charm meets contemporary luxury, making it a top choice for visitors looking for cultural experiences, natural beauty, and fun adventures. In this chapter, we'll explore two must-visit areas: Old San Juan, filled with history and architecture, and the beach districts of Condado and Isla Verde, known for their gorgeous coastlines and exciting nightlife.

Old San Juan: A Window Into The Past

Old San Juan is the cultural and historical centerpiece of Puerto Rico. Its cobblestone streets, colorful buildings, and ancient landmarks tell the story of the island's colonial era. This area, a UNESCO World Heritage site, is one of the best-preserved colonial districts in the Americas and offers countless treasures to explore.

1. Legendary Fortresses and Defenses
- **El Morro (Castillo San Felipe del Morro):**

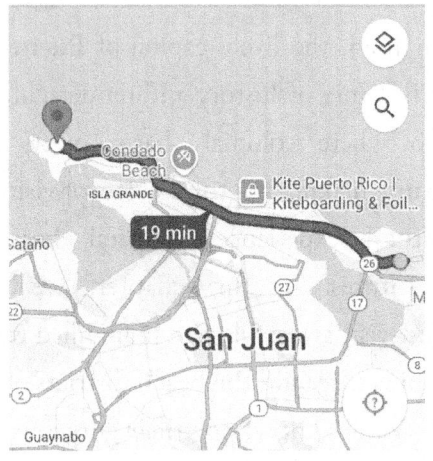

Built in the 1500s, this impressive fortress was designed to protect San Juan from attacks by sea. Its massive walls, sweeping ocean views, and fascinating exhibits make it one of Puerto Rico's top attractions. Visitors can wander the grounds, climb the ramparts, and learn about the fort's role in defending the island during colonial times.

- **San Cristóbal (Castillo San Cristóbal):** This is the largest Spanish fort in the Americas and was built to guard against land-based invasions. Visitors can explore its tunnels, towering walls, and lookout points. The fort also features a museum showcasing maps, artifacts, and displays about life in the Spanish military.

- **City Walls and Batteries:** Scattered around Old San Juan are smaller fortifications like Bateria del Morro and Bateria de la Reina, which were part of the city's defenses. These sites provide a glimpse into Puerto Rico's military history and offer great photo opportunities.

2. Strolling Through the Historic City
- **San Juan Gate (Puerta de San Juan):** Once the main entry point to the city, this historic gate welcomed travelers arriving by sea. Today, it stands as a monument to the city's

rich past. Walking through the gate is like stepping back in time, and the nearby harbor views are stunning, especially at sunset.

- **Paseo del Morro:** This scenic trail runs alongside the old city walls and offers breathtaking views of the ocean. It's a peaceful spot for a walk or a picnic, with plenty of opportunities to see local wildlife and enjoy the coastal breeze.

3. Iconic Buildings and Squares
- **San Juan Cathedral:** This 500-year-old cathedral is a masterpiece of colonial architecture. Inside, you'll find ornate altars, colorful stained glass windows, and the tomb of Juan Ponce de León, the explorer who led Puerto Rico's first European settlement.

- **Plaza de Armas:** As the main square of Old San Juan, this plaza is a lively spot filled with statues, fountains, and local vendors. It's a great place to people-watch, grab a coffee, or explore nearby shops and eateries.

- **Casa Blanca:** Built for Ponce de León's family, this historic house offers a look into colonial life. The surrounding gardens and courtyards create a tranquil space to learn about the island's early settlers.

4. **Museums and Cultural Centers**
   - **Museo de las Américas:**

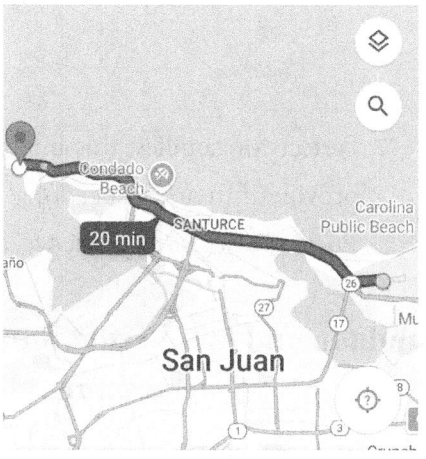

This museum highlights the diverse cultures of the Americas, with exhibits on indigenous traditions, African heritage, and European influences. It's a must-visit for history and art enthusiasts.

- **Children's Museum (Museo del Niño):**

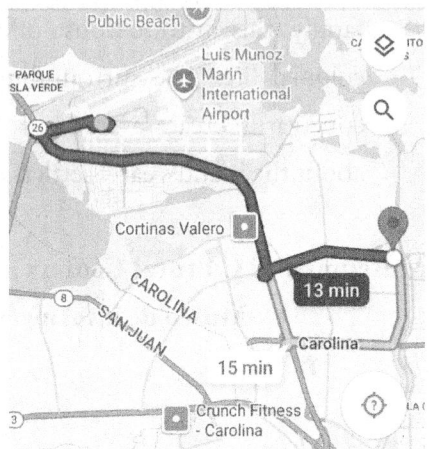

Perfect for families, this interactive museum provides fun and educational exhibits about Puerto Rican history, science, and art.

Condado and Isla Verde: Sun, Sand, and Entertainment

The neighborhoods of Condado and Isla Verde offer a modern, beachy contrast to Old San Juan's historic charm. Known for their sparkling waters and vibrant nightlife, these areas are ideal for relaxing by the sea or enjoying Puerto Rico's lively social scene.

1. Beaches and Watersports
- **Condado Beach:**

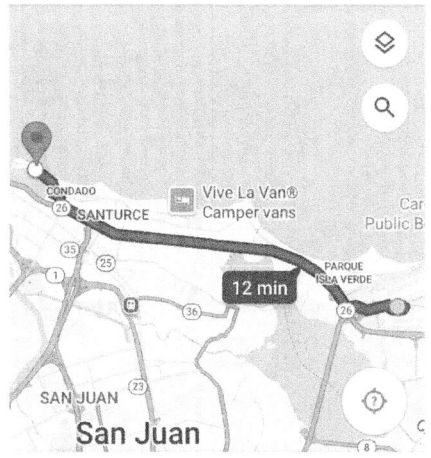

This popular beach is perfect for sunbathing, swimming, or trying out water sports like paddleboarding and jet skiing. Its calm waves and golden sands attract both locals and visitors. Luxury hotels like Condado Vanderbilt and La Concha Resort line the shoreline, offering beachfront dining and rooftop pools.

- **Isla Verde Beach:**

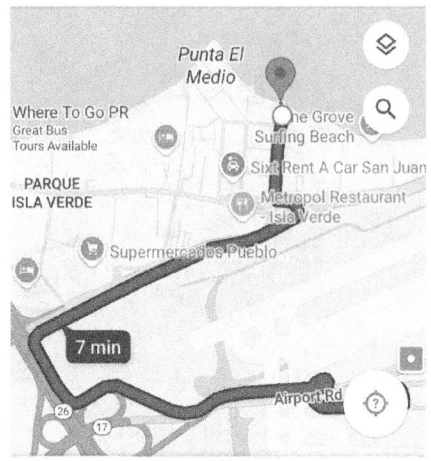

A bit quieter than Condado, Isla Verde is known for its clear waters and laid-back atmosphere. It's a great spot for families, with shallow waters perfect for kids and plenty of space for picnics and relaxing.

2. **Nightlife and Entertainment**
   - **Condado's High-End Scene:** Condado is home to upscale cocktail bars and nightclubs like The Champagne Bar and Oasis Nightclub, where you can enjoy live music and dancing.

   - **Isla Verde's Relaxed Vibe:** In Isla Verde, you'll find cozy beachfront bars and live music venues like Café del Mar, which are ideal for enjoying a casual evening out.

- **La Placita de Santurce:** Located near these districts, this bustling square comes alive at night with food stalls, street performers, and salsa dancing.

3. **Dining Options**
   - **Fine Dining in Condado:** Restaurants like Oceano serve gourmet meals with stunning ocean views, while 1919 Restaurant offers a luxurious dining experience featuring local ingredients.

   - **Casual Eats in Isla Verde:** For a laid-back meal, head to places like Piu Bello, known for Italian dishes, or try local street food at Plaza del Mercado.

Other Highlights Around San Juan

While Old San Juan, Condado, and Isla Verde are the main attractions, there are other must-see places nearby:

- **El Yunque National Forest:** Located a short drive away, this tropical rainforest is full of hiking trails, waterfalls, and lush greenery.

- **Puerto Rico Convention Center:** This modern venue hosts events and is surrounded by restaurants, shops, and open spaces for visitors to enjoy.

CHAPTER 8

DISCOVERING PUERTO RICO'S EAST COAST AND ISLANDS

The eastern side of Puerto Rico is a dream destination for nature enthusiasts and thrill-seekers. It's home to the lush greenery of El Yunque Rainforest and the serene beauty of the islands Vieques and Culebra. This region offers breathtaking landscapes, diverse ecosystems, and incredible adventures. In this chapter, we'll explore the highlights of these stunning locations, including El Yunque's trails and waterfalls and the islands' glowing bioluminescent bays and untouched beaches.

El Yunque Rainforest: A Tropical Gem

El Yunque National Forest is the only tropical rainforest managed by the U.S. National Forest

System. Spanning roughly 29,000 acres, it's one of the Caribbean's most diverse ecosystems. This forest is perfect for hiking, birdwatching, and enjoying nature's beauty. Towering trees, sparkling waterfalls, and rare wildlife make El Yunque a must-see.

1. Hiking Trails for Everyone
El Yunque offers trails suitable for all levels of hikers, each showcasing the forest's natural beauty in different ways.

- **La Mina Trail:** A favorite among visitors, this path leads to La Mina Falls, where you can swim in the refreshing pools beneath the cascading water. Dense greenery lines the trail, making it a scenic walk.

- **El Angelito Trail:** This easy trail is great for families, ending at a peaceful swimming hole surrounded by nature.

- **Mt. Britton Trail:** This steeper trail takes you to the Mt. Britton Tower, an old observation point with stunning views of the rainforest and coastline.

- **Pico El Yunque Trail:** For experienced hikers, this trail leads to one of the highest peaks in the forest, offering panoramic views of the landscape and the Caribbean Sea.

2. Waterfalls in the Forest

The rainforest features several beautiful waterfalls, each with its own charm.

- **La Coca Falls:**

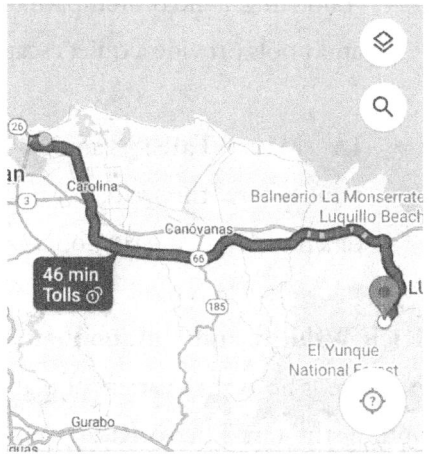

Located near the entrance, this easily accessible waterfall is a striking sight and a popular photo spot.

- **Juan Diego Falls:**

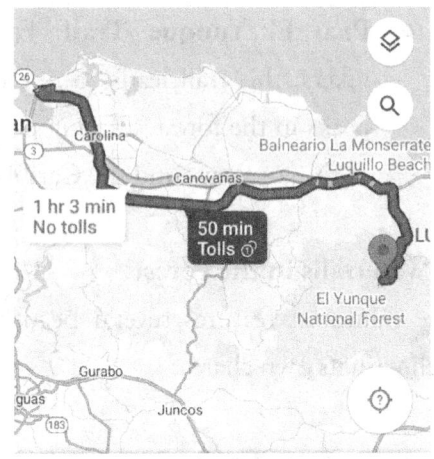

Hidden off the beaten path, these small falls and pools provide a quiet escape for visitors.

- **La Mina Falls:** Famous for its lively atmosphere, this waterfall is ideal for a swim or simply enjoying the cool mist.

3. Rich Wildlife and Unique Plants

El Yunque is home to a variety of plants and animals, including the rare Puerto Rican Parrot and the tiny coquí frog, both symbols of Puerto Rico. Visitors can see vibrant flowers, massive ferns, and ancient trees throughout the forest.

4. Visitor Centers and Guided Tours
- **El Portal Visitor Center:**

Start your visit here to learn about the forest's ecology, history, and efforts to preserve it.

- **Guided Tours:** Local guides offer insights into the forest's history, plants, and animals, providing a deeper understanding of this unique environment.

Vieques And Culebra: Island Getaways

A short ferry or flight from the mainland brings you to the islands of Vieques and Culebra, perfect for relaxation and exploration. Both islands are known for their clear waters, peaceful beaches, and remarkable natural attractions like bioluminescent bays.

Vieques: Peaceful and Pristine
Nicknamed Isla Nena, Vieques is a quiet escape with untouched beaches and fascinating ecological sites.

1. Bioluminescent Bay (Mosquito Bay)
Mosquito Bay, the brightest bioluminescent bay in the world, glows at night thanks to tiny organisms called dinoflagellates.

- **Kayaking at Night:** Paddling through the glowing water under a starry sky is an unforgettable experience. Guides explain the natural phenomenon while helping you navigate the bay.
- **Conservation Efforts:** Visitors are encouraged to use eco-friendly practices, such as avoiding harmful sunscreens, to protect the bay's fragile ecosystem.

2. Stunning Beaches
Vieques offers a variety of beaches, each with its own unique appeal.

- **Playa Negra:**

Known for its striking black sand, this beach provides a dramatic contrast to the turquoise sea.

- **Playa Caracas (Red Beach):**

A family-friendly spot with calm waters and soft white sand, perfect for a relaxing day.

- **Playa La Chiva (Blue Beach):**

This beach is popular for snorkeling, with clear waters and vibrant coral reefs teeming with marine life.

3. Vieques National Wildlife Refuge
Covering much of the island, this refuge protects a variety of habitats, including beaches, mangroves, and wetlands. Visitors can explore the area on foot or by bike while enjoying the peaceful surroundings.

Culebra: Paradise For Beach Lovers
Smaller and quieter than Vieques, Culebra is an ideal destination for anyone looking for serene beaches and vibrant underwater life.

1. Flamenco Beach

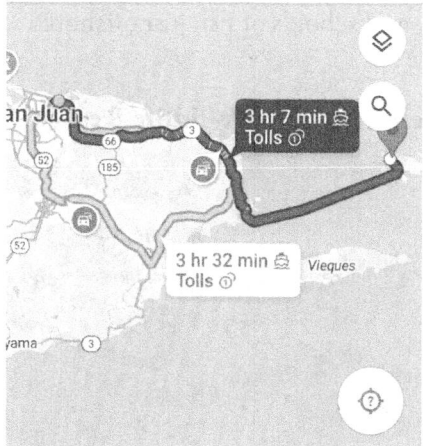

Often ranked among the world's best beaches, Flamenco Beach is known for its soft white sand, clear blue water, and calm waves. The old military tanks on the beach add a touch of history and intrigue.

2. Snorkeling and Diving

Culebra's waters are perfect for snorkeling and diving, with colorful coral reefs and abundant marine life.

- **Tamarindo Beach:** Great for spotting sea turtles, this beach offers calm waters and easy access to reefs.

- **Carlos Rosario Beach:** A secluded spot ideal for snorkeling, featuring vibrant corals and schools of fish just offshore.

3. Culebra National Wildlife Refuge

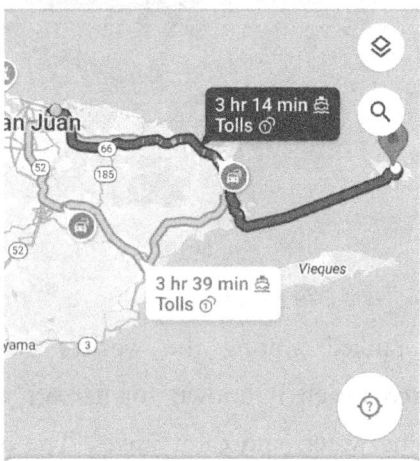

This refuge covers a large portion of the island and is a sanctuary for sea turtles and seabirds. Trails within the refuge offer opportunities for birdwatching and exploring the island's natural beauty.

Tips For Visiting The Islands

- **Getting There:** Ferries from Ceiba and small planes from San Juan provide access to both Vieques and Culebra. Reservations are recommended, especially during busy seasons.

- **Where to Stay:** From cozy inns to luxurious villas, the islands offer accommodations to suit all budgets.

- **What to Pack:** Essentials include reef-safe sunscreen, water shoes, and snorkeling gear to fully enjoy the beaches and bays.

CHAPTER 9

EXPLORING THE SOUTH COAST OF PUERTO RICO

Puerto Rico's southern region is a treasure trove of history, culture, and nature. Known for its laid-back vibe, the area is a refreshing escape from the busy cities of the north. It is home to the historic city of Ponce, the unique ecosystem of the Guanica Dry Forest, and beautiful beaches. Whether you're looking to dive into the island's history or enjoy its natural wonders, the south coast offers something special for everyone.

Ponce: The "Pearl Of The South"

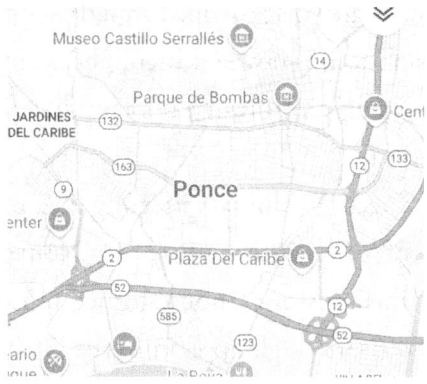

Ponce, Puerto Rico's second-largest city, is rich in culture and history. Nicknamed La Perla del Sur (the Pearl of the South), it boasts elegant colonial and neoclassical buildings, vibrant plazas, and cultural landmarks that highlight its past and present.

1. Exploring Ponce's Historic Heart

Walking through Ponce's old town feels like stepping back in time, with its blend of historic architecture and modern charm.

- **Catedral de Nuestra Señora de Guadalupe:** Located in Plaza Las Delicias, this beautiful cathedral is a mix of Gothic and neoclassical design. It is not only a place of worship but also an architectural gem.

- **Parque de Bombas:** This iconic red-and-black-striped building, once a fire station, is now a museum honoring the city's firefighting history. It's a must-see landmark.

- **Casa Wiechers-Villaronga:** A fine example of early 20th-century Art Nouveau design, this historic house-turned-museum gives visitors a glimpse into the life of Ponce's wealthy families during its golden age.

2. Cultural Landmarks and Museums
Ponce is also a hub for art, history, and archaeology.
- **Museo de Arte de Ponce:** Renowned as one of the best art museums in the Caribbean, it features European and Caribbean art, including the famous painting Flaming June by Frederic Leighton.

- **Museo Histórico de Ponce:** This museum showcases the city's history, from its colonial beginnings to its growth into a cultural hub.

- **Tibes Indigenous Ceremonial Center:** Just outside the city, this archaeological site offers insights into the lives of the island's indigenous Taíno people, with ancient artifacts, burial sites, and ceremonial grounds.

3. La Guancha Boardwalk

Located along the waterfront, La Guancha Boardwalk is a lively gathering spot filled with local food, music, and scenic views.

Food and Drinks: Try traditional snacks like empanadillas or enjoy freshly caught seafood from the kiosks lining the boardwalk.

Activities: Visitors can watch fishermen at work, take a boat ride, or feed the pelicans that flock to the area.

4. Celebrating Ponce's Festivals

Ponce is famous for its colorful celebrations, bringing locals and visitors together to honor the city's traditions.

- **Carnaval de Ponce:** One of the island's most exciting events, this February festival features vibrant parades, traditional vejigante masks, and lively music.

- **Fiestas Patronales:** Every June, the city celebrates its patron saint, St. John the Baptist, with religious processions, music, and cultural activities.

Guanica Dry Forest: A Rare Ecosystem

West of Ponce lies the Guanica Dry Forest, a UNESCO Biosphere Reserve and one of the world's largest dry forests. This unique landscape is a stark contrast to Puerto Rico's lush rainforests.

1. Trails for Every Explorer

The forest has several trails for nature lovers, ranging from easy walks to challenging hikes.

- **Fuerte Caprón Trail:** Hike to the ruins of an old Spanish fort and enjoy sweeping views of the forest and the coast.

- **Ballena Trail:** This trail is ideal for birdwatchers, offering sightings of rare species like the Puerto Rican Nightjar.

- **Cueva Trail:** This short path leads to a limestone cave, a cool and quiet retreat for explorers.

2. Unique Plants and Wildlife

The dry forest is home to a wide variety of plants and animals, some found nowhere else in the world.

- **Flora:** You'll see cacti, acacias, and other drought-tolerant plants thriving in this arid environment.

- **Fauna:** Look out for iguanas, colorful butterflies, and rare species like the Puerto Rican crested toad and the yellow-shouldered blackbird.

Relaxing at Guanica's Beaches

After exploring the forest, unwind at nearby beaches known for their calm waters and picturesque scenery.

- **Playa Santa:** A favorite among locals, this beach has golden sand, clear water, and nearby restaurants serving fresh seafood.

- **Gilligan's Island (Cayo Aurora):** Take a ferry or kayak to this small island, perfect for snorkeling, swimming, or enjoying a picnic under the mangroves.

- **Playa Tamarindo:** This secluded beach is ideal for snorkeling, offering a chance to see colorful coral reefs and marine life.

Tips For Your South Coast Adventure

- **Transportation:** Renting a car is the easiest way to explore the region's attractions and reach hidden gems.

- **Local Cuisine:** Don't miss specialties like roasted pork, fresh fish, and guava-filled pastries.

- **Best Time to Visit:** The dry season, from December to April, is the most comfortable time for outdoor activities and beach days.

CHAPTER 10

EXPLORING PUERTO RICO'S WEST COAST

Puerto Rico's west coast is a beautiful and adventurous part of the island, offering stunning beaches, a strong surfing culture, and unique natural attractions. This region is quieter than San Juan, providing a more laid-back experience. Whether it's the surf town vibe of Rincon, the rugged landscapes of Cabo Rojo, or the lesser-known treasures along the coast, visitors can find a mix of excitement and relaxation.

Rincon: Surfing And Stunning Sunsets

Rincon, also called the "Town of Beautiful Sunsets," is a favorite spot for surfers, beach lovers, and nature enthusiasts. Its connection to the ocean shapes the town's lifestyle, but it also appeals to travelers looking for yoga retreats, art, or tranquil beachside experiences.

1. Surfing Hotspot

Rincon is widely recognized as Puerto Rico's surfing capital, attracting surfers of all skill levels.

Top Surfing Beaches:
- **Domes Beach:** Known for its consistent waves, this beach is a great spot for skilled surfers and hosts major surf competitions.

The unique dome structure near the beach adds character to the area.

- **Maria's Beach:** This location offers strong breaks for experienced surfers and serves as a learning area for beginners through nearby surf schools.

- **Sandy Beach:** With smaller, more manageable waves, this spot is ideal for those just starting out or looking for a more relaxed surfing experience.

Surf Lessons and Rentals: Plenty of local shops provide surfboards, gear, and professional lessons, making it easy for newcomers to dive into the sport.

2. Activities Beyond Surfing

Rincon offers much more than just great waves.

- **Snorkeling and Diving:** Visit the Tres Palmas Marine Reserve to explore colorful coral reefs and spot sea turtles, parrotfish, and other marine life.

- **Whale Watching:** Between January and March, humpback whales pass through the waters off Rincon, offering a spectacular sight for visitors.

- **Punta Higüero Lighthouse:** This historical lighthouse provides sweeping ocean views and is a perfect spot to catch the sunset.

3. Local Culture and Relaxation

Rincon is a creative and peaceful community where visitors can unwind or enjoy cultural activities.

- **Art Walks:** The weekly Rincon Art Walk showcases handmade goods, local art, and live music. It's a fun way to experience the town's creative energy.

- **Yoga and Wellness:** Rincon is known for yoga studios and wellness centers offering classes and retreats for relaxation and mindfulness.

4. Food and Drinks

Rincon's dining options include local favorites and international cuisines. Fresh seafood dishes, like ceviche and shrimp mofongo, are common, and many beachfront restaurants serve cold tropical drinks, perfect for watching the sunset.

Cabo Rojo: Nature's Masterpiece

Cabo Rojo, located in Puerto Rico's southwest, is a destination known for its dramatic cliffs, unique salt flats, and serene beaches. It's a paradise for nature lovers and anyone looking to escape into unspoiled beauty.

1. The Salt Flats
Cabo Rojo's salt flats are a fascinating natural attraction.
- **Pink Hues and Unique Scenery:** The salt flats appear pink and white due to microorganisms and high salt content,

creating a striking visual against the green vegetation and blue skies.

- **Wildlife Refuge:** The surrounding area is a protected habitat for many bird species, including the rare yellow-shouldered blackbird. Trails offer visitors a chance to explore the refuge and spot wildlife.

- **Educational Visits:** The local visitor center provides information on the history of salt production and the ecological importance of the region.

2. Lighthouse and Coastal Cliffs

The Cabo Rojo Lighthouse, also called El Faro Los Morrillos, is one of the area's highlights.

- **Stunning Views:** Perched on a cliff, the lighthouse offers panoramic views of the ocean and rugged coastline, making it a top spot for photos and sunsets.

- **Historical Site:** Built in the 1800s, the lighthouse has helped guide ships for centuries and remains a significant landmark.

- **Hiking Paths:** Trails near the lighthouse lead to secluded beaches and hidden coves, perfect for those seeking a quiet escape.

3. Pristine Beaches

Cabo Rojo is home to some of the most picturesque beaches in Puerto Rico.

- **Playa Sucia (La Playuela):** A quiet, crescent-shaped beach with clear waters and soft sand, ideal for swimming or relaxing.

- **Combate Beach:** A lively beach often visited by locals, it's great for families and offers nearby dining options.

- **Gilligan's Island:** Accessible by kayak or ferry, this small cay features shallow, crystal-clear waters and mangrove trees, perfect for snorkeling and paddleboarding.

4. Outdoor Activities

For those who love outdoor adventures, Cabo Rojo offers plenty to do.

- **Kayaking and Paddleboarding:** Explore the calm waters and mangrove ecosystems by kayak or paddleboard for a peaceful nature experience.

- **Cycling Trails:** Bike trails wind through the region, offering scenic views of the salt flats and coastal areas.

Tips For Visiting The West Coast

- **Getting Around:** A rental car is the best way to explore the region and reach more remote spots.

- **Best Time to Visit:** December through April offers the best weather for beach days and outdoor activities.

- **Essentials to Pack:** Bring sunscreen, sturdy shoes for hiking, and snorkeling gear to make the most of your visit.

- **Food to Try:** Don't miss local specialties like crab empanadas (empanadas de jueyes) and freshly caught fish, along with locally brewed craft beers.

CHAPTER 11

EXPLORING PUERTO RICO'S CENTRAL MOUNTAINS

Puerto Rico's central mountains, also called the Cordillera Central, are a hidden treasure. They give visitors the chance to experience the island's true rural charm, fascinating history, and stunning natural beauty. The area is full of breathtaking landscapes, rich culture, and exciting outdoor activities, making it the perfect place for those wanting to explore Puerto Rico away from the usual tourist spots. Two of the most popular towns in this region, Utuado and Jayuya, each offer something unique—whether it's lush coffee farms, adventure sports, indigenous history, or scenic drives.

Utuado: Coffee Farms And Outdoor Adventures

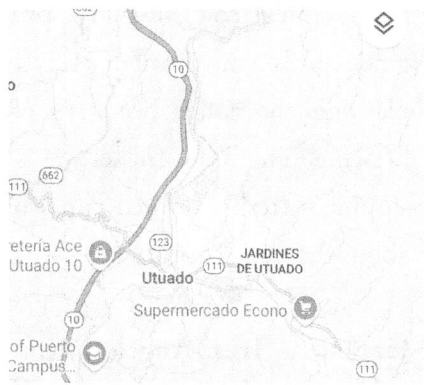

Nestled in the middle of Puerto Rico's mountains, Utuado is a town surrounded by dense forests and towering peaks. Known as the "Town of the River," Utuado is famous for its coffee heritage and beautiful natural surroundings. If you're a coffee lover, enjoy outdoor activities, or want to learn more about Puerto Rico's rural life, Utuado offers a truly authentic experience.

1. Coffee Culture in Utuado
Utuado is a major hub for coffee production in Puerto Rico, and the town's history is closely tied to the coffee industry.

- **Hacienda San Pedro:** This historic coffee farm offers visitors a chance to learn about the island's coffee-making process. Tour guides walk you through everything—from planting the coffee beans to roasting and brewing. The beautiful setting is perfect for sipping a freshly brewed cup while learning about the farm's history.

- **Hacienda Tres Ángeles:** Known for its sustainable farming practices, this eco-friendly coffee farm offers guided tours to teach visitors about environmentally conscious coffee production. You'll get to see the entire process and sample some of the region's finest coffee.

- **Coffee Tasting:** Many of Utuado's local coffee shops serve some of the best coffee on the island. If you're passionate about coffee, this is your chance to try Puerto Rican coffee in its purest form—strong, rich, and full of history.

2. Outdoor Adventures

Utuado is a great place for outdoor activities, with its mountainous terrain and rivers providing perfect opportunities for hiking and adventure sports.

- **Cueva Ventana (Window Cave):** One of Puerto Rico's most famous natural spots, this limestone cave on a cliff offers incredible views of the Río Grande de Arecibo valley. The cave's entrance frames a picturesque "window" to the valley below, making it a must-see for nature lovers.

- **Tanamá River Adventures:** If you're looking for excitement, the Tanamá River has it all—river tubing, rappelling, kayaking, and cave exploration. You can explore hidden caves, navigate river rapids, and experience the island's rugged beauty up close.

- **Hiking Trails:** Utuado is home to several hiking trails that pass through lush forests and up steep peaks. Whether you're after a relaxing walk or a more challenging hike, you'll find plenty of options. Some trails also lead to waterfalls and scenic viewpoints.

3. Cultural and Historical Sites

Utuado is full of places that tell the story of Puerto Rico's past, including its indigenous roots.

- **Tibes Indigenous Ceremonial Center:** Just outside Utuado, the Tibes Ceremonial Center provides a glimpse into the history of Puerto Rico's Taíno people. The site includes ceremonial grounds, petroglyphs, and burial sites, offering a fascinating look into the island's early cultures.

- **Local Museums:** Utuado has several small museums that explore the town's history and culture. The Museum of the History of Utuado features exhibits on the town's development, while the Museum of Sacred Art showcases religious artifacts and artwork.

Jayuya: Indigenous History and Scenic Views

Jayuya, located in the central mountains, celebrates its indigenous Taíno heritage and stunning natural beauty. Known as the "Indigenous Capital of Puerto Rico," Jayuya is a peaceful place filled with historical sites and scenic roads that let visitors dive into Puerto Rico's natural and cultural history.

1. Taíno Heritage and History
Jayuya is deeply connected to Puerto Rico's indigenous past, and it is the ideal spot to learn about the Taíno people, the island's original inhabitants.

- **Caguana Indigenous Ceremonial Park:** One of Puerto Rico's most important archaeological sites, Caguana is home to ancient stone plazas and ball courts used by the Taíno people for ceremonies. Visitors can walk through the site and learn about Taíno culture and rituals. The park also has a visitor center with exhibits about Taíno history.

- **Museo El Cemí:** In Jayuya, this museum is dedicated to the Taíno people. Designed like a Taíno deity figure (cemí), the museum features artifacts such as pottery and ceremonial objects. Visitors can learn about Taíno beliefs, their social structure, and their legacy in Puerto Rican culture.

- **Petroglyphs and Rock Art:** The area around Jayuya is dotted with ancient rock carvings made by the Taíno. These petroglyphs, found along hiking trails and riverbeds, offer fascinating insight into the Taíno's artistic expressions and beliefs.

2. Scenic Drives and Views

The central mountains are known for their winding roads and breathtaking views, and Jayuya is no different. Whether you're driving or hiking, the scenery will leave you in awe.

- **Toro Negro State Forest:** A lush, protected forest near Jayuya, Toro Negro is perfect for nature lovers. The forest offers trails, waterfalls, and rich wildlife. It's also home to Cerro de Punta, Puerto Rico's tallest mountain, where visitors can enjoy sweeping views of the surrounding valleys and mountains.

- **Mirador Orocovis-Villalba:** This lookout point, located at the border of Jayuya and Orocovis, offers expansive views of the central mountains. The sight of the green hills stretching far into the distance is a stunning representation of Puerto Rico's natural beauty.

- **La Piedra Escrita:** A culturally significant rock, La Piedra Escrita is carved with Taíno petroglyphs. It is located along the Río Saliente and can be reached via a short hike. The rock is a peaceful place to learn about the Taíno and enjoy the quiet of the forest.

3. Festivals and Traditions

Jayuya celebrates its indigenous heritage through lively festivals and cultural events.

- **Festival Indígena (Indigenous Festival):** This annual festival in November celebrates Jayuya's Taíno roots with music, dance, and traditional arts. Visitors can enjoy Taíno-inspired performances, local crafts, and delicious Puerto Rican food. It's a fun and educational event that brings the island's native history to life.

- **Craft Workshops:** Jayuya also offers cultural workshops where you can learn to make traditional Puerto Rican crafts like pottery and weaving. These hands-on activities help you connect with the local culture.

4. Natural Beauty

Jayuya is also home to some of Puerto Rico's most beautiful natural spots, including waterfalls and rivers.

- **Salto de Doña Juana:** A stunning waterfall just outside of Jayuya, Salto de Doña Juana falls into a calm pool, making it a perfect spot for swimming, taking photos, or relaxing in nature.

- **Río Saliente:** This crystal-clear river is ideal for swimming or picnicking. The surrounding forest provides a peaceful atmosphere, and its secluded location makes it a perfect place for unwinding.

Tips For Visiting The Central Mountains

- **Transportation:** Renting a car is essential for exploring the mountainous areas. Roads can be narrow and winding, so be ready for a scenic drive that can also be challenging at times.

- **Best Time to Visit:** The best time to visit the central mountains is during the dry season, from December to April, when the weather is perfect for outdoor activities.

- **What to Pack:** Bring comfortable hiking shoes, light clothes, and a rain jacket. Weather in the mountains can change quickly, so it's important to be prepared for anything.

- **Local Food:** While in Jayuya and Utuado, be sure to try local dishes like pasteles (Puerto Rican tamales), guanime (cornmeal dumplings), and, of course, freshly brewed coffee from the mountains.

CHAPTER 12

STAYING SAFE IN PUERTO RICO

Puerto Rico is a stunning island known for its beautiful landscapes, rich culture, and friendly locals. However, just like any travel destination, it's important to take safety precautions to enjoy a stress-free trip. Whether you're traveling on your own, with a partner, or as a family, knowing how to stay safe and avoiding common scams can make your visit more enjoyable. This chapter provides practical tips to help you have a secure and memorable experience on the island.

Safety Tips For Solo Travelers, Families, And Couples

Travelers face different safety challenges depending on how they travel. Below are some specific tips for solo adventurers, families, and couples to help keep everyone safe.

Solo Travelers

Traveling alone is exciting and gives you plenty of freedom, but it's wise to take some extra precautions.

- **Stay in Touch:** Let someone back home know your travel plans. Send updates via text or email so they know where you are.

- **Avoid Lonely Areas:** While Puerto Rico has many beautiful beaches and trails, avoid isolated places, especially after sunset. Stick to well-visited spots for safety.

- **Don't Stand Out:** Dress casually and avoid displaying expensive items like jewelry or cameras. Learning a few Spanish phrases can also help you blend in and communicate better with locals.

- **Pick Secure Accommodations:** Stay in well-rated areas such as Condado, Old San Juan, or Isla Verde. Read reviews to ensure your lodging is in a safe neighborhood.

- **Verify Rideshares:** If using Uber or similar services, double-check that the driver and vehicle match the information in the app.

Families

Traveling with children requires careful planning to make the trip both fun and safe.

- **Pack Essentials:** Bring sunscreen, bug spray, and a basic first-aid kit for small problems like cuts or sunburns.

- **Choose Safe Beaches:** Some beaches don't have lifeguards, so opt for family-friendly spots like Luquillo Beach or Flamenco Beach, which are calmer and safer for kids.

- **Stay Together:** If visiting crowded places like festivals or markets, make sure children know a meeting spot in case you get separated. Younger kids can wear wristbands with contact details.

- **Teach Wildlife Safety:** Remind kids not to touch unknown animals, as they could carry diseases or react aggressively.

Couples

Couples can enjoy the romance of Puerto Rico while staying aware of their surroundings.

- **Protect Your Belongings:** Use the hotel safe to store important items like passports, cash, and jewelry. Don't leave valuables unattended at the beach.

- **Be Smart on Nights Out:** Stick to well-known restaurants and bars in busy tourist areas. Monitor your drinks and avoid excessive alcohol.

- **Stay Alert:** Even while enjoying romantic walks, be mindful of your surroundings, especially in less populated or dimly lit areas.

Common Scams And How To Avoid Them

As with many tourist hotspots, Puerto Rico has its share of scams. Being aware of these schemes can help you avoid unnecessary problems.

1. Overpriced or Fake Taxis

Some drivers may inflate fares or operate without proper licensing.

How to Avoid: Use Uber for clear pricing. If taking a taxi, agree on the cost before starting the ride or confirm the meter is on.

2. Unofficial Tour Guides

Scammers might offer cheap tours that are unsafe or don't happen at all.

How to Avoid: Book excursions through trusted companies or your hotel. Look up reviews online before committing.

3. Pickpocketing

Thieves often target tourists in busy areas, working in groups to distract and steal.

How to Avoid: Carry your belongings in a secure bag with zippers. Be alert in crowded places and avoid keeping valuables in back pockets.

4. ATM Fraud

Some ATMs may be tampered with to steal card details.

How to Avoid: Use ATMs located inside banks. Check the card reader for signs of tampering before inserting your card.

5. Fake Vacation Rentals
Some online listings for rental properties may be scams, where the property either doesn't exist or isn't available.

How to Avoid: Stick to reputable platforms like Airbnb or book directly through hotels. Never pay upfront using wire transfers or cash.

6. Pushy Helpers
Some people may offer help, like carrying luggage, and then demand a tip or steal from you.

How to Avoid: Politely decline assistance from strangers unless they are authorized staff.

7. Inflated Restaurant Bills
Certain restaurants may add hidden charges to your bill or inflate prices for tourists.

How to Avoid: Always ask to see a menu with prices before ordering. Check your bill carefully for unexpected charges.

8. Fake Emergencies

Scammers might approach you with a made-up story, such as claiming they need money for an emergency.

How to Avoid: Decline politely and move on. If you want to help, direct them to local authorities instead of giving money.

General Safety Tips For Puerto Rico

- **Know Emergency Numbers:** For police, medical, or fire emergencies, dial 911.

- **Get Travel Insurance:** Insurance can cover you for accidents, health issues, or trip cancellations.

- **Avoid Flashy Items:** Keep valuables like jewelry, cash, or electronics out of sight to avoid attention.

- **Watch the Weather:** Hurricane season is from June to November. Keep track of local weather updates and follow official advice during storms.

- **Trust Your Instincts:** If something doesn't feel right, don't hesitate to leave or avoid the situation. Your safety is more important than politeness.

CHAPTER 13

PACKING AND GETTING READY

Traveling to Puerto Rico isn't just about booking your flights and finding a place to stay—it's also about packing wisely and being prepared for anything. Whether you're heading to the beach, hiking in the rainforest, or walking through historical sites, this chapter will help you pack the right items, get ready for different activities, and understand why travel insurance and having emergency contacts are important.

What To Pack For Different Activities

Puerto Rico offers a mix of beaches, forests, and city life, so it's important to pack for all kinds of experiences. Here's a guide to help you prepare based on your plans.

Beach and Water Fun

Puerto Rico is known for its beautiful beaches, like Flamenco Beach and Luquillo Beach, and exciting water activities like snorkeling and kayaking.
- **Swimwear:** Pack a couple of swimsuits so you always have a dry one.
- **Beach Towel:** Bring a lightweight towel that dries quickly.
- **Sun Protection:** Don't forget sunscreen (reef-safe if snorkeling), sunglasses, a hat, and SPF lip balm.
- **Water Shoes:** These are great for rocky areas and tide pools.
- **Waterproof Bag:** Keep valuables like your phone and camera safe near the water.
- **Snorkel Gear:** If you'll snorkel a lot, bring your own gear for convenience.

Hiking and Outdoor Adventures

For hiking in El Yunque or exploring natural reserves, you'll need a few essentials.
- **Sturdy Shoes:** Wear comfortable, durable shoes with good grip.
- **Light Clothes:** Breathable, moisture-wicking clothes are best for the humid weather.

- **Bug Repellent:** Protect yourself from mosquitoes in forested areas.
- **Water Bottle:** Bring a reusable bottle to stay hydrated.
- **Rain Gear:** A lightweight rain jacket or poncho is handy for unexpected rain showers.
- **Daypack:** Use a small backpack to carry snacks, water, and other essentials.

City Sightseeing and Cultural Experiences

San Juan, Ponce, and other cities offer rich history and culture.

- **Comfortable Shoes:** Choose supportive footwear for walking on cobblestone streets.
- **Casual Clothes:** Bring neat, casual outfits for museums and dining out.
- **Guidebook or App:** A guidebook or travel app can help you explore.
- **Reusable Bag:** This can be useful for souvenirs or market finds.
- **Power Bank:** Keep your devices charged while you're out and about.

Evenings and Special Events

Puerto Rico has lively nightlife and occasional festivals, so pack for these too.

- **Dressy Outfit:** Include at least one nice outfit for fancy dinners or events.
- **Comfortable Night Shoes:** Stylish but comfy shoes are perfect for evenings out.
- **Light Jacket or Wrap:** Some indoor places may have strong air conditioning.

Travel Insurance And Emergency Contacts

Being prepared for unexpected situations can save you stress while traveling.

Travel Insurance

Travel insurance is a smart choice for any trip.

- **Medical Help:** Make sure your plan covers medical emergencies and evacuation.
- **Trip Cancellation:** Protect your trip in case it gets canceled or delayed.
- **Lost Luggage:** Choose coverage for lost or delayed bags.

- **Adventure Sports:** If you're trying activities like snorkeling or zip-lining, check if your insurance covers them.

Emergency Contacts

Keep important contact numbers handy in case you need them.

- **Local Emergencies:** Dial 911 in Puerto Rico for police, fire, or medical help.
- **Insurance Contact:** Have your insurance company's phone number ready.
- **Hotel Details:** Write down your hotel's address and phone number.
- **Friends or Family:** Save their contact details in case your phone battery dies.
- **Consulate Information:** If you're not a U.S. citizen, find the contact for your country's consulate in San Juan.

Extra Packing Tips

- **Pack Light:** Only bring what you need. You can buy most items on the island if necessary.
- **Medication:** Take enough prescription medicine for your trip and a small first-aid kit.

- **Cash and Cards:** While cards are widely accepted, carry some cash for small purchases.
- **Documents:** Keep copies of your ID, passport, travel insurance, and itinerary.
- **Weather Prep:** Expect warm weather but pack for occasional rain.

CHAPTER 14

UNDERSTANDING PUERTO RICAN CULTURE

Exploring Puerto Rico is more enjoyable when you take the time to understand its culture. The island's lively traditions, welcoming people, and unique mix of Spanish, Taino, and African influences create a vibrant atmosphere. Knowing some basic Spanish and local customs can make communication smoother and show your respect for the culture. This chapter will help you learn useful Spanish phrases and provide tips on what to do—and avoid—when interacting with locals.

Simple Spanish Phrases For Visitors

Although many Puerto Ricans speak English, especially in tourist areas, learning some Spanish can make your trip more enjoyable. Locals appreciate it when visitors try to speak their language, even if it's just a few words.

Greetings And Polite Words

Hello: Hola
Good morning: Buenos días
Good afternoon: Buenas tardes
Good evening/night: Buenas noches
Goodbye: Adiós
Please: Por favor
Thank you: Gracias
You're welcome: De nada
Excuse me/Sorry: Perdón or Disculpe
Yes: Sí
No: No

Common Questions

How are you?: ¿Cómo está? (formal) / ¿Cómo estás? (informal)

What is your name?: ¿Cómo se llama? (formal) / ¿Cómo te llamas? (informal)

Where is...?: ¿Dónde está...?

Example: "Where is the bathroom?": ¿Dónde está el baño?

How much does it cost?: ¿Cuánto cuesta?

Do you speak English?: ¿Habla inglés? (formal) / ¿Hablas inglés? (informal)

Helpful Words For Travel
Hotel: Hotel
Airport: Aeropuerto
Taxi: Taxi
Beach: Playa
Water: Agua
Food: Comida
Help!: ¡Ayuda!

Shopping and Dining Phrases
I would like...: Quisiera...

Example: "I would like a coffee": Quisiera un café.

The check, please: La cuenta, por favor.

Can I have this?: ¿Puedo tener esto?

How much is this?: ¿Cuánto cuesta esto?

Practicing these phrases before your trip or using a language app can help you communicate with confidence.

Tips For Puerto Rican Etiquette

Understanding local customs can make your visit more enjoyable and leave a good impression. Here are some things to do and avoid during your trip.

What to Do
1. Be Friendly and Greet People:
Puerto Ricans are warm and sociable. A smile and a polite "Hola" or "Buenos días" go a long way. In social settings, a handshake or a light cheek kiss is common, depending on the relationship.

2. Respect Older People:
Elders are treated with respect in Puerto Rican culture. Use polite language and formal titles when addressing them.

3. Try Local Foods:
Sample dishes like mofongo, arroz con gandules, tostones, and lechón. Complimenting the food is a great way to connect with the locals.

4. Enjoy the Music and Dance:
Puerto Rico is known for its music styles like salsa, reggaeton, and bomba. Don't hesitate to join in if

there's dancing—it's a fun way to experience the island's lively spirit.

5. Be Patient:
Life on the island tends to move at a slower pace. Whether waiting for food or dealing with minor delays, staying patient will help you enjoy the relaxed atmosphere.

6. Support Local Businesses:
Visit local markets, eat at small restaurants, and buy handmade souvenirs. This not only supports the community but also gives you a more authentic experience.

7. Learn About the History:
Exploring places like Old San Juan, El Morro, or La Fortaleza can deepen your appreciation for Puerto Rico's culture and heritage.

What Not to Do
1. Don't Be Too Loud:
While Puerto Ricans enjoy lively conversations, being overly loud in public spaces can be seen as impolite.

2. Don't Assume Everyone Speaks English:

Many people are bilingual, but it's considerate to ask if someone speaks English or to try using a little Spanish.

3. Don't Ignore Local Traditions:
Be respectful of religious or cultural practices. For example, dress appropriately when visiting churches or sacred sites.

4. Avoid Comparing Puerto Rico to the Mainland:
Puerto Ricans take pride in their culture and identity. Avoid making comments that might come across as dismissive.

5. Don't Litter:
Puerto Ricans value their beautiful environment. Always clean up after yourself at beaches, parks, or city streets.

6. Don't Rush Conversations:
Social interactions are meaningful in Puerto Rico. Take your time and enjoy the opportunity to chat with locals.

7. Don't Be Too Formal at Gatherings:

While manners are important, Puerto Rican hospitality is relaxed and informal. Being too stiff might make you seem unapproachable.

CHAPTER 15

SAMPLE ITINERARIES

Visiting Puerto Rico can be as laid-back or adventurous as you'd like. The island's compact size makes it easy to see a lot in just a few days, while its diversity ensures there's plenty to explore during longer stays. These itineraries outline ideas for short trips and extended vacations, helping you plan an unforgettable adventure.

3-Day Weekend in San Juan

If you only have a long weekend, San Juan offers the perfect mix of history, beaches, and nightlife.

Day 1: Discover Old San Juan
Morning:
Start your day with a traditional breakfast at Cafetería Mallorca, known for its delicious pastries and coffee.

Wander through Old San Juan, enjoying the colorful buildings and cobblestone streets.

Visit Castillo San Felipe del Morro, a historic fortress with stunning ocean views.

Afternoon:
Savor lunch at Raíces, which serves Puerto Rican classics like mofongo.

Stroll along Paseo de la Princesa, a scenic walkway with fountains and local vendors.

Tour Castillo de San Cristóbal, another fort with impressive views and hidden passages.

Evening:
Have dinner at a rooftop restaurant such as Aire Rooftop Bar for panoramic sunset views.

End your day with drinks and live music at La Factoría, a globally recognized bar.

Day 2: Relax at the Beach
Morning:
Spend your morning at Condado Beach or Ocean Park Beach, ideal for sunbathing and swimming.

For some fun, try paddleboarding or jet skiing.

Afternoon:
Grab a casual meal at El Alambique Beach Lounge or a food truck near the beach.

Explore the Santurce neighborhood, famous for its vibrant murals and street art.

Evening:
Enjoy dinner at Santaella, which offers a mix of modern and traditional Puerto Rican cuisine.

If it's Thursday or Friday, head to La Placita, a bustling plaza with music, dancing, and nightlife.

Day 3: Visit El Yunque
Morning:
Take a short drive to El Yunque National Forest, about 45 minutes from San Juan.

Hike trails like La Mina Falls or Angelito Trail to enjoy rainforest views and waterfalls.

Afternoon:

On your way back, stop by Luquillo Beach and grab a bite from the popular Kioskos de Luquillo.

Return to San Juan for some last-minute shopping or relaxation before heading to the airport.

5-Day East Coast Adventure

This itinerary lets you explore lush forests, beautiful beaches, and glowing bioluminescent waters.

Day 1: Arrive in San Juan

Settle into your hotel and enjoy an easy evening.

Take a walk along the Condado Lagoon or enjoy fine dining at 1919 Restaurant.

Day 2: El Yunque and Luquillo Beach

Spend your morning hiking El Yunque, exploring its trails, waterfalls, and scenic views.

Relax at Luquillo Beach in the afternoon, then sample snacks from the Kioskos de Luquillo.

Day 3: Fajardo and Bioluminescent Bay

Morning: Take a boat tour to Icacos Island, where you can snorkel and enjoy the beach.

Afternoon: Visit Las Cabezas de San Juan Nature Reserve and the Fajardo Lighthouse.

Evening: Experience the glowing waters of Laguna Grande, one of the island's bioluminescent bays.

Day 4: Vieques or Culebra
Take a ferry or flight to one of these nearby islands.

In Vieques, visit Mosquito Bay or relax on Playa Negra.

In Culebra, enjoy the crystal-clear waters of Flamenco Beach or snorkel at Tamarindo Beach.

Day 5: Return to San Juan
Spend a quiet morning by the beach or exploring local shops before heading back to San Juan.

7-Day Island Road Trip

Take a week to discover the entire island, exploring cities, beaches, and natural wonders.

Day 1: Tour San Juan's historic and modern areas.

Day 2: Visit Cueva del Indio and Camuy River Cave Park on the north coast.

Day 3: Head west to Rincón for surfing and beachside sunsets.

Day 4: See the Cabo Rojo Lighthouse and the nearby Salt Flats. Take a boat ride to La Parguera Bioluminescent Bay at night.

Day 5: Explore Ponce, visiting the Parque de Bombas and the Ponce Art Museum.

Day 6: Travel into the central mountains for coffee tours and hikes in Toro Negro State Forest.

Day 7: Return to San Juan, revisiting favorite spots or relaxing before departure.

14-Day Full Puerto Rico Experience

A two-week trip offers the chance to dive deep into Puerto Rican culture and nature.

Week 1:

Explore San Juan, El Yunque, and Luquillo.

Visit Arecibo, Camuy Caves, and Rincón.

Spend time in Cabo Rojo and Ponce.

Week 2:

Enjoy coffee farms and hiking in the central mountains.

Relax on Vieques or Culebra.

Discover the Guánica Dry Forest and Gilligan's Island.

Wrap up with a visit to Fajardo and nearby islands.

CHAPTER 16

HELPFUL CONTACTS AND WEBSITES

Having the right contact details and websites at your fingertips can make your trip to Puerto Rico much smoother and safer. From finding tourist information to knowing emergency contacts, being prepared can help you stay on track. This section provides essential resources to keep you informed and connected during your stay.

Tourist Information Centers

Puerto Rico has several tourist centers around the island, offering valuable information such as maps, brochures, local suggestions, and details about attractions. These centers are staffed by locals who can help with specific questions and provide useful recommendations.

San Juan – Old San Juan Visitor Center
Location: In the center of Old San Juan, near the cruise terminal.

Services: Maps, guides, details on historic sites, local events, restaurants, and transportation.

Contact: +1 (787) 722-1709

Website: www.prtourism.com

Ponce – Ponce Visitor Center

Location: Plaza Las Delicias, Ponce.

Services: Information on Ponce's landmarks, beaches, and cultural spots like the Ponce Art Museum and Parque de Bombas.

Contact: +1 (787) 843-5052

Website: www.visitponce.com

Fajardo – East Coast Visitor Center

Location: Near Fajardo's marina, close to the ferry stations for Vieques and Culebra.

Services: Offers info on beaches, water activities, and trips to nearby islands and reserves.

Contact: +1 (787) 863-0730

Website: www.discoverpuertorico.com

Arecibo – Arecibo Observatory Visitor Center
Location: Along the northern coast of Puerto Rico.

Services: Information about the Arecibo Observatory and nearby natural sites. Tours available.

Contact: +1 (787) 878-2612

Website: www.naic.edu

Rincón – Rincón Visitor Center
Location: In Rincón, a well-known surf town on the west coast.

Services: Info on surfing spots, eco-tourism, beaches, and nature reserves.

Contact: +1 (787) 823-0510

Website: www.rinconpr.org

Emergency Numbers And Services

It's important to have the right contacts in case of emergencies or unexpected events while traveling in Puerto Rico. Here are the key numbers to keep on hand:

Emergency Numbers
Police: 911 (For crimes or accidents)

Fire Department: 911 (For fire-related emergencies)

Medical Help: 911 (For ambulances or medical emergencies)

Coast Guard (For sea emergencies): +1 (787) 724-0800

Roadside Assistance: 1-800-228-0118 (For car breakdowns or flat tires)

Hospitals
Puerto Rico Medical Center (Centro Médico de Puerto Rico)
Location: Río Piedras, San Juan
Contact: +1 (787) 758-2525

Hospital Pavia – Ponce
Location: Ponce
Contact: +1 (787) 843-4747

Hospital San Francisco – Fajardo
Location: Fajardo
Contact: +1 (787) 863-5022

Pharmacies

Farmacias El Amal
Location: Various locations across Puerto Rico
Contact: +1 (787) 722-4130
Website: www.farmaciaselamal.com

Walgreens
Location: Available in major cities like San Juan, Ponce, and Bayamón
Website: www.walgreens.com

Other Important Services

Roadside Assistance – AAA Puerto Rico
Contact: +1 (787) 775-8989
Website: www.pr.aaa.com

Lost and Found (Puerto Rico Tourism Company)
Contact: +1 (787) 722-1709

Weather Alerts

National Weather Service (NWS) Puerto Rico
Contact: +1 (787) 253-4525
Website: www.weather.gov/sanjuan

Tourism And Safety Assistance

If you need information on local attractions, events, or safety tips, the Puerto Rico Tourism Company is a great resource. They offer a wealth of information to help plan your trip and keep you safe during your visit.

Puerto Rico Tourism Company
Contact: +1 (787) 722-1709
Website: www.discoverpuertorico.com

By keeping these essential contacts and websites handy, you can have a safer and more enjoyable trip to Puerto Rico. Whether you need help with travel plans, are seeking emergency services, or just want to learn more about the island's attractions, these resources will ensure you stay connected and informed throughout your visit.

CONCLUSION

Puerto Rico is a place that combines stunning landscapes, rich history, vibrant traditions, and friendly locals. This book has taken you through the island's variety of experiences, from the lively streets of San Juan to the peaceful shores of Vieques and the lush greenery of El Yunque. Each chapter shared useful information about the island's culture, history, must-visit spots, travel tips, and sample itineraries to help you create the perfect trip for your needs.

From learning about Puerto Rico's past and picking up basic Spanish phrases to discovering hidden attractions and savoring local dishes, this guide was designed to make your visit easy and memorable. Whether you're planning a weekend getaway, a deeper exploration, or a cultural experience, the tips and resources here will help you make the most of your journey.

Take in the island's lively spirit, honor its customs, and connect with its welcoming people. As you travel through Puerto Rico, use this guide to uncover all the unique and special things it has to offer. Enjoy your trip and create unforgettable memories!

Made in the USA
Monee, IL
29 December 2024